MW01222965

The Self-Care Code

15 Essential Rituals for Busy Professionals

By Faraz Mubarik

Copyright © 2023 by Faraz Mubarik

All rights reserved. No part of this book may be reproduced or transmitted in any form or by any means, electronic or mechanical, including photocopying, recording, or by any information storage and retrieval system, without permission in writing from the author.

Disclaimer:

The author and publisher have made every effort to ensure the accuracy of the information within this book. However, the information contained in this book is sold without warranty, either express or implied. The author and publisher will not be held liable for any damages caused or alleged to be caused directly or indirectly by this book.

Faraz Mubarik

London, UK

ISBN: 9798399819280

Imprint: Independently published

"Self-care is not a luxury; it's an essential code that unlocks your potential and guarantees your success."

Dedication

To my beloved father, Mubarik Ahmed,

You were more than a father to me; you were a guiding light, an inspiration, and a constant source of love and support. Your presence may no longer be with us, but your spirit lives on in every page of this book. Your unshaken belief in the power of self-care and the pursuit of personal growth continues to inspire me every day.

This book, "The Self-Care Code: 15 Essential Rituals for Busy Professionals," is dedicated to your memory. Your knowledge, generosity, and unstoppable commitment to your family and job formed the person I am today. Your passing has taught me the value of cherishing each moment and cultivating our own well-being in the midst of life's pressures.

May your legacy live on via the knowledge offered on these pages, changing the lives of others, and inspiring them to prioritise self-care, achieve balance, and realise their full potential. You will forever remain in my heart, and I am grateful for the enormous impact that you have had on my life.

With eternal love and gratitude,

Faraz Mubarik

Table of Contents

Introduction

"The Self-Care Code: 15 Essential Rituals for Busy Professionals." It is simple for professionals to get caught up in the never-ending cycle of work, responsibilities, and the constant pressure to achieve more in today's hectic and demanding world. Amid this turmoil, it is essential to remember that your own well-being is as vital as any other aspect of your life.

This book is a comprehensive guide designed to help busy professionals like yourself prioritise self-care and discover the keys to a more balanced, gratifying, and joyous life. We recognise the unique difficulties you face and the limited time you can devote to yourself. Therefore, we have hand-picked 15 essential rituals that can be easily incorporated into your hectic schedule, allowing you to reclaim your well-being and flourish in all areas.

Each chapter of this book explores a distinct aspect of self-care and provides strategies, techniques, and actionable actions to help you develop a sustainable self-care practise. From fostering physical vitality to managing tension and cultivating emotional well-being, we cover a broad range of topics that are essential for your overall health.

"The Self-Care Code" goes beyond occasional indulgences and fast remedies. It involves establishing a strong foundation of self-care that becomes an integral part of your daily existence. By implementing these essential rituals, you will not only improve your personal well-being but also your professional effectiveness. The benefits of self-care extend far beyond the individual; they reverberate through your relationships, work, and quality of life.

Whether you are a high-powered executive, an entrepreneur, or a dedicated professional in any discipline, this book will assist you on your path to holistic wellness. The time has come to break the cycle of exhaustion, tension, and overwhelm. It's time to put yourself first and invest in your most valuable asset: yourself.

So, are you ready to crack the self-care code? Are you ready to unlock the secrets to a healthier, happier, and more fulfilling life? If the answer is yes, then let's move forward together on this journey of development. Discover the essential rituals that will enable you to find balance, cultivate resilience, and reclaim your well-being amidst the hectic pace of your career.

"The Self-Care Code: 15 Essential Rituals for Busy Professionals." Simply tells you that, It is time to prioritise yourself and redefine your life narrative.

"Invest in yourself. It's the best investment you'll ever make."

Chapter 1

Self-Care in a Busy Life

Busy professionals in today's fast-paced environment sometimes find themselves managing several duties and facing constant demands on their time and energy. In this chapter, we will go deeply into the concept of self-care and its significant relevance in the context of a busy lifestyle. By understanding the importance of self-care, readers will gain a comprehensive insight into how it can positively impact their well-being and overall quality of life.

Defining Self-Care:

Self-care is defined as a wide variety of deliberate actions and practises that people participate in to care for their physical, emotional, mental, and spiritual well-being. It entails actively devoting time and energy to nurturing oneself and cultivating a good connection with oneself. Self-care is not a selfish act; rather, it is necessary for preserving balance, managing stress, and stimulating personal growth.

Self-care may take many different shapes for various people because it is extremely personalised. Exercise, healthy nutrition, getting adequate sleep, practising relaxation methods, engaging in hobbies and interests, obtaining emotional support, creating boundaries, and engaging in self-reflection are all examples of activities that might be included. The idea is to do things that nourish and restore your body, mind, and soul.

Recognising the Consequences of Self-Care Neglect:

Individuals who overlook their self-care needs may suffer negative implications for their general well-being. Chronic tiredness, diminished immune function, increased susceptibility to sickness, and decreased vigour are all symptoms of physical neglect. Emotional neglect can result in increased stress, anxiety, emotional fatigue, and decreased emotional resilience. Neglect of the mind can lead to trouble concentrating, poor cognitive function, creative stagnation, and impaired problem-solving ability. Spiritual neglect may leave people feeling detached, unhappy, and without purpose or meaning in their lives.

Neglecting self-care has consequences not just for people individually, but also for their work life. It can result in reduced efficiency, burnout, poor decision-making, strained relationships with coworkers, and a decreased sense of fulfilment and happiness at work.

Creating a Foundation for Self-Care Priorities:

To effectively incorporate self-care into a stressful life, a firm foundation that prioritises personal well-being must be established. This foundation involves recognising the importance of self-care and making a conscious decision to prioritise it as an essential component of one's daily routine.

First and foremost, it is critical to recognise that self-care is neither a luxury nor a selfish act. It is required for healthy physical, emotional, and mental wellness. It is critical to change one's thinking and ideas about self-care. Let go of any guilt or social messages that indicate self-care is foolish or worthless. Recognise that by taking care of yourself, you will be better able to complete your obligations and present your best self in your personal as well as your professional life.

Making a self-care strategy can help provide a foundation for prioritising self-care. Begin by recognising your specific self-care requirements as well as the activities that offer you joy, relaxation, and fulfilment. Create a list of self-care practises that speak to you and are consistent with your beliefs and priorities. Consider the various aspects of self-care - physical, emotional, mental, and spiritual - and aim for balance in each.

Creating a self-care routine that works for you. This could mean setting aside time in your calendar for self-care activities, such as a morning meditation, a lunchtime stroll, or an evening relaxation practise. Set limits and explain your self-care priorities to everyone around you so that they understand and appreciate your need for time for yourself.

Remember that taking care of yourself is an ongoing practise. It demands dedication, consistency, and adaptation. Be open to trying new self-care practises and adapting them as your needs and circumstances change. Accept self-compassion and give yourself permission to prioritise your own well-being without judgement or perfectionism.

Setting a foundation for valuing self-care sets the groundwork for a long-term and beneficial self-care journey that can benefit many elements of your hectic lifestyle.

Chapter 2

Assessing Your Current Practises

Before starting a journey to improve the way you take care of yourself, it's important to look at what you're already doing. This chapter will walk you through a thorough self-assessment process that will help you see how well you are taking care of yourself right now. By knowing your abilities and where you can improve, you can make smart choices and plan for self-care that is tailored to your needs and goals.

Reflecting on Your Self-Care Habits:

Take a moment to think about how you take care of yourself now. Think about the physical, social, mental, and spiritual aspects of self-care and ask yourself the following:

Physical Self-Care:

- How often do I do things that are good for my health and well-being that are physical? Do I prioritise exercise and movement in my daily routine?

- Do I pay attention to what I eat and choose foods that give my body what it needs? • How well do I prioritise hydration and water intake?
- How well do I control my sleep schedule and make sure I get enough rest each night?

Emotional Self-Care:

• Am I aware of my feelings and able to share them in a healthy way? Do I work on being aware of my own emotions?

• Do I have strategies for managing stress and emotional well-being? How do I deal with unpleasant emotions?

• Do I show myself kindness and take care of myself when I'm feeling stressed out or mentally drained?

Mental Self-Care:

• How do I take care of my mental health and keep my mind clear? Do I do things that keep my mind active and help me think quickly?

• Am I aware of my feelings, and do I talk to myself in a good way? How well do I deal with mental tiredness and anxiety?

• Do I take time to do things that help me relax and clear my mind, like meditation or hobbies?

Spiritual Self-Care:

• How attached do I feel to my principles, beliefs, and sense of purpose? Do I do things that make me feel good and give me a sense of purpose?

• Do I take time to think about myself and look inward? How often do I say thank you and try to be more aware?

• Do I do spiritual things or look for situations that fit with what I believe and what I value?

Identifying Places to Get Better:

Based on what you've learned about yourself, figure out where you think your self-care practises may be missing or could be better. Think about the following questions:

• What self-care activities do I always forget to do or find hard to put first in my busy life?

• Am I overlooking or not paying enough attention to certain parts of self-care?

• Do I often feel burned out, stressed out, or emotionally exhausted?

• Are there any outside causes or barriers that make it hard for me to take care of myself on a regular basis?

By being honest about your self-care habits and finding places to improve, you can learn a lot about the parts of self-care that need your attention. This awareness is the first step towards making changes that matter and building a better self-care routine.

Setting Goals for Self-Care:

Once you've figured out what you need to work on, it's time to set self-care goals that fit your wants and goals. Think about the following:

• Prioritise: Choose one or two areas of self-care or specific tasks that need your attention right away and put them at the top of your self-care plan.

• Make sure your goals are clear and measurable. Instead of a vague goal like "exercise more," set a goal like "be physically active for at least 30 minutes at least three times a week."

• Realistic: Make sure your goals are doable with the way you live and work now. Having unrealistic expectations can cause frustration and resentment.

• Steady Steps: Break your goals down into smaller steps that you can take. This makes it easy to take care of yourself and build habits that will last.

Making an Action Plan for Self-Care:

With your goals in mind, make a thorough plan for taking care of yourself that includes the steps and strategies you will use to meet your needs. Think about the following things:

• Commitment of Time: Find out how much time you can set aside each day or week for self-care. Be reasonable and flexible, considering the other things you must do.

• Tasks: Choose tasks for self-care in line with your goals and preferences. Include a variety of self-care tasks from different areas to improve your well-being.

Schedule: Put things that help you take care of yourself on your daily or weekly schedule. Think of them as meetings with yourself that you can't break.

• Support: Find any tools, services, or people who can help you keep up with your self-care routine. This could be done with the help of accountability friends, self-care apps, or advice from a professional.

Monitoring Constantly and Making Changes:

Don't forget that self-care is an ongoing process. As your life changes, so will your need for self-care. Make it a habit to look at your self-care habits, goals, and action plan on a regular basis and make changes as needed. Stay open to new ways to take care of yourself and change your method as needed to make sure you keep growing and staying healthy.

Conclusion:

Assessing your current self-care practises is a critical step in enhancing your well-being. You may give yourself an opportunity to prioritise self-care and make changes in your hectic life by reflecting on behaviours, identifying areas for improvement, defining self-care objectives, and developing an action plan. Keep in mind that self-care is an ongoing process; by regularly monitoring and changing your approaches, you may create a self-care habit that serves you well over the long term.

Chapter 3

Rituals for Physical Well-being

The practise of self-care that prioritises one's physical wellness has far-reaching effects on one's health and happiness. In this chapter, we will examine several behaviours that can help busy professionals maintain their physical health. You can increase your physical health, energy, and enthusiasm by implementing these habits into your daily life.

Prioritising Exercise

The foundation of physical health is a routine exercise. There are many ways in which it improves our physiological and psychological well-being. Every aspect of your health, from your heart and lungs to your muscles and bones to your weight and the risk of chronic disease, can benefit from a regular exercise routine. To make exercise a top priority, consider the following methods:

Finding Activities You Enjoy: One of the key factors in sticking to an exercise routine is finding activities that you genuinely enjoy. When deciding on a fitness routine, it's important to take personal tastes into account. Jogging, hiking, and bicycling are all enjoyable pursuits that can be done outside, which may appeal to you. Try taking a dance lesson or signing up for a team sport if you enjoy social gatherings. Find what makes you happy and makes you look forward to working out, and stick with it.

Scheduling Exercise Sessions: Treat exercise as an important appointment in your calendar. Schedule your workouts the same way you would any other important appointment or event in your life. This could involve getting up earlier in the morning to exercise, going for a stroll during your lunch break, or scheduling an evening gym session. When you make exercise a fixed part of your schedule, you're more likely to look forward to it and stick with it.

Incorporating: Movement Throughout the Day: Although scheduled exercise sessions are beneficial, it's also crucial to work movement into your day in less formal ways. Look for ways to include more exercise into your everyday routine. If you want to get healthier, you can do things like use the stairs instead of the lift, park further away from your destination, or take advantage of your breaks to stretch and move around. These brief periods of exercise can have significant benefits for your health.

Joining a Group: Fitness class or working out with a friend can increase motivation, ensure you hold each other accountable, and make exercise more fun. Look for a training partner who is interested in the same things you are. You can keep each other motivated and turn working out into a fun group outing. You can also find like-minded people and form a supportive exercise community by enrolling in group fitness courses or recreational sports leagues.

Prioritising Consistency over Intensity: Consistency is key when it comes to exercise. Moderate activity performed on a regular basis is preferable to vigorous exercise performed infrequently. Exercises like brisk walking and cycling count towards your weekly goal of at least 150 minutes of aerobic activity at a moderate intensity. If you can't devote a full day to it, divide it up into several shorter blocks. Keep in mind that maintaining a regular fitness routine is the key to seeing lasting results.

Tracking Progress: Keep records of your workouts and improvements to keep yourself motivated and aware of your achievements. Keep track of your workouts by using a fitness tracker, an app on your smartphone, or even just a notepad. Motivate yourself to keep exercising on a regular basis by celebrating small victories along the way.

Remember, if you have any preexisting medical illnesses or concerns, you should talk to your doctor before beginning any new fitness programme. You can get tailored advice and make sure your fitness routine is safe and effective.

Physical fitness, energy levels, stress management, and general health and happiness can all benefit from making exercise a daily priority. Pick activities that fascinate you, make time for them regularly and have fun doing them. Exercising on a regular basis is like building the groundwork for a happy, healthy, and successful future.

Nourishing Your Body with Healthy Eating Habits

A proper diet is critical for physical well-being. Consuming nutritious foods gives your body the nutrients, vitamins, and minerals it requires to function properly. You may improve your general health, maintain a healthy weight, increase your energy levels, and support your body's many systems by adopting healthy eating habits. Here are some ideas for nourishing your body through healthy eating habits:

Eating a Balanced Diet: consisting of a variety of fruits, vegetables, whole cereals, lean proteins, and healthy fats. Each food group contains critical nutrients that benefit your overall health. Include colourful fruits and vegetables to acquire a variety of vitamins, minerals, and antioxidants. Whole grains, such as quinoa, brown rice, and whole wheat bread, have a higher fibre content. Choose lean proteins like chicken, fish, beans, and tofu, as well as healthy fat sources like avocados, almonds, and olive oil. To meet your body's nutritional demands, aim for a balanced plate that includes a variety of these food groups.

Meal Preparation and Planning: Planning and preparing your meals ahead of time will help you make better choices and save time on hectic days. Make time every week to plan your meals, make a grocery list, and prepare ingredients or pre-cook meals. A well-planned meal plan decreases your dependency on processed or unhealthy convenience meals and ensures that nutritional selections are easily available. Weekend batch cooking or meal prep can also be advantageous because it allows you to have pre-portioned meals or components ready to assemble during the week.

Mindful Eating: Use mindful eating to cultivate a healthier relationship with food and make conscious decisions about what and how you consume. Slow down and focus on your food selections, eating carefully and savouring each bite. Listen to your body's hunger and fullness cues and eat until you're satisfied but not stuffed. Avoid distractions such as screens or work-related activities when eating and instead concentrate on the sensory experience of the food. You can acquire a stronger appreciation for food, improve digestion, and make more conscious food choices by practising mindful eating.

Hydration: Hydration is an important part of good nutrition. Drink enough water throughout the day to keep your body running smoothly. Carry a water bottle with you and make a habit of drinking water on a regular basis, especially during moments of physical activity or when you're thirsty. Water regulates body temperature, facilitates digestion, delivers nutrients, and improves general health.

To add flavour to plain water, try infusing it with slices of citrus fruits, cucumber, or mint leaves.

Portion Control: Pay attention to portion sizes to ensure you're getting enough food to meet your body's demands. Understand optimal portion amounts for different food groups by using visual clues or measuring equipment. Avoid eating in excess and pay attention to your body's hunger and fullness cues. Smaller, more balanced meals and nutritious snacks can help reduce overeating and ensure consistent energy levels throughout the day.

Mindful Food Choices: Read food labels and comprehend the contents and nutritional value of the foods you consume to make educated food choices. When feasible, choose whole, minimally processed foods and reduce your intake of sugary drinks, processed snacks, and foods high in saturated fats and sodium. Concentrate on nutrient-dense foods that provide a diverse range of important nutrients and promote overall wellness.

Remember that nutritious food is a long-term commitment, not a hard, restricting diet. Allow yourself a little room for occasional indulgences while keeping your eating habits under control overall. A consultation with a trained dietitian or nutritionist can provide specific guidance based on your individual nutritional needs and goals.

Adopting good eating habits provides your body with the resources it requires for optimal health. A well-balanced diet promotes physical well-being, increases energy, and leads to a healthier and more lively way of life.

Embracing Restorative Sleep

Sleep is an essential component of physical health. It gives our bodies a chance to relax, refuel, and recover. Maintaining good health, cognitive function, emotional well-being, and general vitality requires adequate sleep. Here are some techniques for embracing restorative sleep:

Creating a Soothing Bedtime Ritual: Establishing a soothing bedtime ritual helps signal to your body that it is time to wind down and prepare for sleep. Engage in relaxing and calming activities such as reading a book, taking a warm bath, gently stretching, or listening to peaceful music. Following the same routine every night signals to your body that it's time to sleep, which is important.

Making Your Bedroom Sleep-Friendly: Make your bedroom sleep heaven by optimising the sleeping environment. Make sure that the space is dark, silent, and at a comfortable temperature. To block out any unpleasant light, use blackout curtains or an eye mask, earplugs or white noise generators to drown out noise disturbances, and a comfy mattress and pillows that suit your body's demands. Consider eliminating electronic gadgets from your bedroom, such as smartphones and tablets, because the blue light emitted by screens can disrupt the production of melatonin, the hormone that governs sleep.

Prioritise A Consistent Sleep Schedule: Maintaining a consistent sleep schedule is critical for regulating your body's internal clock, also known as the circadian rhythm. Even on weekends, try to go to bed and wake up at the same time every day. Consistency encourages your body's normal sleep-wake cycle, making it easier to fall asleep and wake up feeling refreshed. If you need to change your sleep schedule, do so gradually to give your body time to adapt to the new pattern.

Managing Stress Before Bed: Excessive stress might impair your ability to fall asleep and stay asleep. Use relaxation techniques before going to bed to help quiet your mind and body. Deep breathing techniques, meditation, moderate yoga, or journaling may be used to relieve racing thoughts or worries. Activities that induce relaxation and help you unwind can dramatically improve your sleep quality.

Creating a Digital Detox: The blue light that cell phones, tablets, and computers emit may interfere with your sleep patterns. Create a digital detox habit before bedtime by turning off screens at least one hour before going to bed. Instead, relax by reading a book, listening to gentle music, or participating in a peaceful pastime. This helps your mind prepare for sleep and reduces your exposure to stimulating screens, which might interfere with your ability to fall asleep.

Sleep Hygiene Optimisation: Sleep hygiene refers to the behaviours and practises that promote healthy sleep. Some suggestions for improving your sleep hygiene include:

- Creating a relaxing sleep environment: Make your bedroom cool, dark, and devoid of distractions.
- Limit or avoid stimulants: Caffeine and nicotine can interfere with your ability to fall asleep.
- Limiting daily naps: If you have trouble falling asleep at night, restrict your daytime naps or keep them short and early in the day.
- Regular physical activity: Regular physical activity can help you sleep better, but avoid extreme exercise close to bedtime because it can raise awareness.
- Avoiding large meals and fluids close to bedtime: Eating large meals or drinking significant amounts of fluids close to bedtime might cause sleep disruption owing to digestion or repeated trips to the toilet.

Conclusion:

Prioritising physical well-being rituals is critical for busy professionals looking to improve their overall health and strength. You may increase your energy levels, manage stress, and lower your risk of chronic diseases by implementing these rituals into your daily routine. Keep in mind that tiny, persistent acts build up to big long-term effects. Choose rituals that speak to you and commit to doing them on a regular basis. Adopting physical well-being routines will help you on your path to a happier, more balanced life.

Chapter 4

Rituals for Emotional Balance

For busy professionals, emotional well-being is an essential component of self-care. Taking care of your mental health not only assists you in navigating the difficulties of a hectic lifestyle, but it also increases your overall pleasure and fulfilment. In this chapter, we will look at three crucial rituals for emotional balance. Practising mindfulness and self-awareness, cultivating gratitude and positive thinking, and effective stress management practises.

Mindfulness and Self-Awareness Practise

Mindfulness practise and self-awareness cultivation are basic routines for obtaining emotional balance. These activities help you gain a better knowledge of your thoughts, feelings, and reactions, giving you more clarity and the ability to respond to situations in a more conscious and constructive manner. Here are some methods for incorporating mindfulness and self-awareness into your daily life:

Mindful Breathing: Mindful breathing is a simple yet effective method for bringing your focus back to the present moment. Look for a quiet area where you can sit comfortably. Close your eyes and take a few deep breaths to get in touch with yourself. Concentrate on the sensation of your breath as you inhale and exhale. Take note of how air enters and exits your body, how your belly or chest rises and falls, and any other physical sensations related to your breath. Whenever your thought drifts, bring it back to your breath. This practise promotes inner peace by calming the mind, and increasing self-awareness.

Body Scan Meditation: Body scan meditation is a practise that involves bringing your awareness to different regions of your body in a systematic manner. Find a quiet and comfortable location to sit or lie down. Close your eyes and focus your concentration on the top of your head. Any sensations, tensions, or areas of relaxation in that area should be noted. Slowly transfer your focus down your body, starting with your forehead and ending with your face, neck, shoulders, arms, chest, abdomen, hips, legs, and feet. Observe any sensations without passing judgement or feeling compelled to change them. This practise improves body awareness, relieves tension, and allows you to connect with your physical self more deeply.

Daily Check-ins: Spend a few minutes each day checking in with yourself. Find a quiet area where you can sit comfortably and without distractions. Close your eyes and look inside yourself. Any thoughts, feelings, or bodily sensations that arise should be noted. Allow yourself to completely experience and recognise them without judgement. Take mental and emotional notes on how you're feeling. Are there any reoccurring themes or patterns? This daily self-reflection practise allows you to become more aware of your inner experiences, recognise areas of tension or discomfort, and respond to your needs with compassion and self-care.

Mindful Eating: Mindful eating is the practise of devoting complete attention to the eating experience. We typically eat on the move or while multitasking in our fast-paced lifestyles, which can lead to mindless eating and a disconnect from our bodies' hunger and satiety cues. Choose a meal or snack and create a peaceful and focused dining setting to practise mindful eating. Take a moment to savour your food's colours, textures, and fragrances. Slowly chew each bite, savouring the flavours and sensations in your mouth. Pay heed to your body's hunger and fullness signs. This practise promotes a healthier relationship with food, increases enjoyment of eating, and increases self-awareness of your body's nutritional requirements.

By adopting these mindfulness and self-awareness behaviours into your everyday routine, you can improve your sense of presence, self-awareness, and emotional balance. These routines help you develop a compassionate and nonjudgmental awareness of your thoughts, emotions, and physical sensations, allowing you to handle the obstacles of a hectic professional life with greater ease.

Cultivating Gratitude and Positive Thinking

Cultivating gratitude and developing a positive thinking mindset are strong practises that can dramatically improve your emotional well-being. They assist in shifting your emphasis to the positive parts of your life, cultivating a sense of gratitude, and promoting a more cheerful view. Here are some methods for cultivating thankfulness and good thinking:

Gratitude Journaling: Gratitude journaling is a simple and powerful practise that entails regularly writing down things for which you are grateful. Set aside a few minutes each day, preferably in the morning or evening, to think about the good things in your life. Write down three to five things for which you are grateful, such as helpful relationships, joyful events, successes, or even simple pleasures like a warm cup of tea or a gorgeous sunset. In your entries, be specific and descriptive. This practise generates a sense of abundance and cultivates a thankful mindset by helping you shift your emphasis to the good.

Positive Affirmations: Positive affirmations are empowering comments about yourself that confirm positive characteristics, attitudes, or intentions. Make a list of affirmations that speak to you and reflect the aspects of your life that you wish to improve. For example, you could say, "I am capable of handling challenges with grace and resilience" or "I am worthy of love and happiness." With conviction and belief, repeat these affirmations daily, either in front of a mirror or in your head. This exercise rewires your mental processes, increases self-confidence, and promotes a positive mindset.

Acts of Kindness: Showing kindness to others is an effective method to promote gratitude and a good attitude. In your daily lives, look for ways to assist or uplift people. It can be as simple as a kind word, a helpful hand, or a modest token of gratitude. Kindness not only has a beneficial impact on others, but it also causes you to feel grateful and happy. By concentrating on distributing kindness, you can divert your attention away from negativity and build a sense of connectivity and happiness.

Surrounding Yourself with Positivity: Take a thorough look at the people, situations, and material you often expose yourself to. Positive influences can have a significant impact on your mental well-being. Seek out partnerships and friendships with people who are encouraging and supportive of you. Make your home and workplace environments that promote positivity and nourish your well-being. Also, be aware of the media you consume, such as social media, news, and entertainment. Select stuff that is uplifting, motivating, and consistent with your ideals.

Negative Thought Reframing: Negative ideas can have a big impact on your emotional state and overall well-being. Experiment with changing negative beliefs into more optimistic or realistic ones. Pause and explore any unpleasant thoughts that come to mind. Replace it with a more positive or balanced thought to challenge its accuracy. If you notice yourself thinking, "I always fail at everything," rephrase it as "I am learning and growing through every experience, and I have achieved many successes in the past." This change in the way you think helps you form a habit of positive thought and gives you a more upbeat view.

You can improve self-awareness, embrace gratitude and positive thinking, and effectively manage stress by adopting these emotional balance practises. These practises promote emotional well-being while also providing you with the resilience and inner resources you need to prosper in your hectic professional life. Remember to be kind to yourself as you adopt these rituals into your daily routine and allow them to become a natural part of your schedule.

Stress Management Techniques That Work

Stress is an unavoidable aspect of life, particularly for working professionals. How you handle and cope with stress, on the other hand, can have a significant impact on your emotional well-being. In this section, we will look at effective stress management approaches that can help you navigate stress and lessen its harmful consequences. You may foster emotional balance and resilience in the face of adversity by using these approaches. Here are some ideas for incorporating into your regular routine:

Exercise and Physical Activity: One of the most effective strategies to manage stress is to engage in regular exercise and physical activity. Physical activity promotes the release of endorphins, the body's natural mood-boosting compounds that promote well-being and reduce stress levels. Find a workout or activity that you enjoy, such as walking, jogging, dancing, yoga, or swimming, and include it in your daily routine. Aim for at least 30 minutes of moderate-intensity exercise most days of the week.

Mind-Body Practises: Mind-body practises, such as yoga, tai chi, and qigong, integrate physical movement, breathwork, and mindfulness to promote relaxation and stress reduction. These exercises assist you in connecting with your body, releasing stress, and cultivating a sense of serenity. Set aside time each week to engage in a mind-body practise that speaks to you. You can attend a local class, use online tutorials, or use mobile apps to help you with these practises.

Time Management and Prioritisation: Time management and prioritisation are critical for stress reduction. It's easy to grow nervous and anxious when you're swamped with various duties and commitments. To prioritise your tasks, start by making a to-do list or using a digital task management application. Determine the most important and urgent tasks and divide them into smaller, more doable segments. You may reduce stress and enhance productivity by organising your time and focusing on critical tasks.

Stress Reduction Tactics: You can incorporate numerous stress reduction tactics into your everyday routine to encourage relaxation and stress relief. Deep breathing techniques, such as diaphragmatic breathing or box breathing, aid in the activation of the body's relaxation response and the relaxing of the mind. To relieve tension, progressive muscle relaxation includes tensing and relaxing each muscle group in your body. Meditation, guided imagery, and visualisation techniques can also help to reduce stress and promote inner calm. Try out different things to find out what works best for you.

Self-Care and Leisure Activities: Self-care and leisure activities are essential for stress management. Make time in your calendar for hobbies that bring you joy and relaxation. Hobbies, creative interests, spending time with loved ones, or engaging in activities that refresh and rejuvenate you are examples of this. Prioritise self-care activities including bathing, reading, listening to music, and practising mindfulness. These activities provide a welcome vacation from the demands of work and aid in the restoration of balance in your life.

Social Support: Seeking help from others is critical for stress management. Reach out to trusted friends, family members, or colleagues who can listen and offer advice. Participate in meaningful discussions, share your experiences, and seek guidance or encouragement. Connecting with others reduces feelings of isolation and provides a support network during difficult times.

Remember that everyone's stress management needs are unique, so it's critical to experiment and find ways that work for you. Experiment with the above tips to see how they affect your stress levels and overall well-being. You may better manage stress, improve emotional balance, and live a healthier and happier life by implementing effective stress management practises into your daily routine.

Conclusion

The practises of mindfulness, gratitude, and stress management that are outlined in this chapter can be used as rituals for restoring mental balance. Emotional health, optimism, and fortitude may all be improved via regular practise of these techniques. Keep in mind that achieving and maintaining emotional equilibrium is a lifelong process that may provide significant rewards if you put in the time and effort.

"Your self-care routine should be as unique as you are."

Chapter 5

Rituals for Mental Clarity

Maintaining mental clarity is critical for busy professionals to survive and perform at their best in today's fast-paced world. This chapter looks at routines and practises that can help you focus, improve cognitive function, and cultivate mental clarity while dealing with the pressures of your work life. By adopting these routines into your daily routine, you can improve your mental health and productivity. Let's look at the fundamental mental clarity rituals:

Considering Mindfulness and Meditation

Meditation and mindfulness are effective habits for improving mental clarity, focus, and overall well-being. In this section, we will look at the benefits of meditation and mindfulness and how to incorporate them into your daily life.

Meditation Explained:

Meditation is an activity in which the mind is trained to create a state of concentrated awareness and inner tranquilly. You can improve mental clarity, reduce stress, and boost cognitive performance by developing a regular meditation practise. Here's how to work meditation into your daily routine:

a. Find a Quiet Place: Find a peaceful and comfortable location where you can sit or lie down without being distracted. It might be a designated meditation area in your house, a tranquil spot in nature, or even a quiet room at work.

b. Set Aside Time: Begin with a moderate amount of time, such as 5-10 minutes, and gradually increase it as you grow more familiar with the practise. Aim for at least one meditation session per day, preferably in the morning to set a positive tone for the day or in the evening to unwind and relax.

c. Choose a Technique: There are several meditation techniques to try, including focused attention, loving-kindness meditation, and mindfulness meditation. Experiment with many strategies to find the one that works best for you.

d. Concentrate on Your Breath: Concentrating on your breath is a simple and efficient meditation practise. Close your eyes, take slow, deep breaths, and pay attention to how your breath enters and exits your body. When your mind slips, gently bring it back to your breath.

e. Accept Non-Judgment: Thoughts and emotions may arise during meditation. Simply observe them with interest and without judgement rather than becoming engrossed in them or judging yourself. Allow them to move through your awareness without becoming attached to them.

Mindfulness Training in Daily Life:

Being fully present in the moment entails paying attention to your thoughts, feelings, and experiences without judgement. You can cultivate mental clarity and improve your capacity to focus by adding mindfulness to your daily life. Here are some ways to develop mindfulness:

a. Mindful Eating involves paying attention to the flavours, textures, and aromas of the food you consume. Chew slowly and thoroughly. Take note of the feelings in your body as well as any ideas or emotions that come during the meal. Eating thoughtfully can increase your appreciation of food while also promoting a sense of tranquilly.

b. Mindful Movement: Walk, practise yoga, or do Tai Chi with a concentration on the present moment. Pay attention to your bodily sensations, the rhythm of your breath, and your body's movements. This helps to ground your consciousness in the present moment and lends mindfulness to your motions.

c. Mindful Pause: Throughout the day, take short mindful pauses. Pause for a few moments, close your eyes, and focus on your breathing. Any tension or stress in your body should be actively released with each exhale. This practise allows you to refocus and refresh by breaking the cycle of constant activity.

d. Mindful Listening and Communication: When participating in conversations, practise active listening. Give the speaker your undivided attention, fully hearing their words and observing their nonverbal signs. Respond with clarity and sensitivity to build genuine connections and minimise misunderstandings.

e. Mindful Technology Use: Be aware of how you use technology and how it affects your mental clarity. Set boundaries and "tech-free" times to reduce distractions and make room for focused work or leisure. When utilising digital gadgets, practise mindful browsing by being aware of your aim and purpose.

Consistency is required when incorporating meditation and mindfulness into your daily practise, as well as determination. Begin with simple steps and progressively increase the length and frequency of your actions. You will benefit from increased mental clarity, improved focus, and a general sense of well-being over time.

Journaling for Mental Reflection and Processing

Journaling is a very effective tool for mental reflection and processing. It offers an organised and safe environment in which you can communicate your thoughts, emotions, and experiences. In this section, we will look at the benefits of journaling and how to incorporate it into your self-care practise.

Understanding the Positive Effects of Journaling

Journaling has several advantages for mental clarity and well-being. Here are some significant benefits:

a. Writing down your thoughts and emotions allows you to release pent-up emotions and decreases brain clutter. It allows you to acquire clarity and perspective by providing an outlet for processing difficult emotions such as tension, anxiety, or despair.

b. Self-Reflection: Journaling promotes self-reflection by allowing you to examine your beliefs, values, and experiences. It enables you to explore deeper into your thoughts and acquire insights on patterns, triggers, and opportunities for personal development.

c. Problem-Solving: By journaling, you can examine difficulties, brainstorm solutions, and explore many points of view. Writing about difficulties can help you obtain a new perspective and devise effective solutions for overcoming them.

d. Increased Self-Awareness: Journaling on a regular basis increases self-awareness by drawing attention to your thoughts, emotions, and behaviours. It assists you in identifying patterns, triggers, and areas for development, leading to a better understanding of yourself.

e. Stress Reduction: Journaling serves as a method of self-care and stress relief. It provides a safe area for people to express their worries, fears, and concerns, thereby lessening their emotional weight and fostering a sense of relaxation and serenity.

Beginning Your Journaling Journey:

a. Choose a Journal: Find a journal or notebook that speaks to you. Choose a format that works for you, whether it's a simple notepad, a nicely bound diary, or a digital journaling software.

b. Establish a Regular Writing Schedule: Allocate a particular time each day or week for journaling. Establishing a journaling habit requires consistency. Find a time that works for you, whether it's in the morning, around lunch, or before bed.

c. Make a Non-Judgmental Environment: Remember that journaling is a personal and private practise. Make a safe area where you can freely express yourself without fear of judgement or criticism. Allow yourself to be open and honest in your writing.

d. Choose a Writing Style: Journaling can be done in a variety of ways. You can write freely and spontaneously, allowing your thoughts to flow freely and uninhibitedly. To explore specific subjects or emotions, you can also use prompts or guided journaling exercises. Experiment with several styles to see what works best for you.

e. When journaling, try for free-flowing writing rather than editing or censoring oneself. Allow your thoughts and emotions to flow freely onto the paper. This enables genuine self-expression and deeper exploration.

Journaling Prompts and Techniques:

a. Gratitude Journaling: Begin each day by writing down three things you're grateful for. Consider the positive parts of your life, no matter how big or tiny. This practise promotes mental clarity and cultivates a positive outlook.

b. Set a timer for a set amount of time, such as 10-15 minutes, and write continually without pausing or censoring yourself. Allow your thoughts to flow freely, allowing your mind to wander and explore various ideas and feelings.

c. Reflective Journaling: Select a specific event, setting, or experience to reflect on. Write about your feelings, emotions, and insights concerning that specific occurrence. To drive your exploration, ask yourself introspective questions like, "What did I learn from this experience?" or "How did it impact my well-being?"

d. Journaling for Problem-Solving: When faced with a challenge or making a difficult decision, consider journaling as a problem-solving tool. Write down the problem or choice at hand, consider the many options, balance the benefits and drawbacks, and express viable solutions. This technique aids in the clarification of your thinking and the clarity of your decision-making.

e. Future Self Journaling: Imagine yourself a month, a year, or five years in the future. Write a diary entry from the perspective of your future self, reflecting on your desired successes, progress, and experiences. This activity promotes a sense of purpose and helps you link your behaviours with your long-term goals.

Conclusion:

Journaling as part of your self-care practise can substantially improve mental clarity and self-reflection. Journaling gives a space for introspection, emotional release, and problem-solving, whether you write freely, use prompts, or apply specialised strategies. Find a journaling practise that speaks to you and commit to writing sessions on a regular basis. You can get useful insights, improve self-awareness, and negotiate the intricacies of your busy professional life with greater mental clarity by writing.

Mental Stimulation through Creative Activities

Engaging in creative activities is an excellent way to stimulate your mind, inspire your creativity, and improve your general well-being. In this section, we will look at the benefits of creative activities and how to incorporate them into your self-care regimen.

Understanding the Advantages of Creativity:

Participating in creative hobbies might improve your mental clarity and well-being significantly. Here are several significant advantages:

a. Mental Stimulation: Creative activities stimulate neural networks and improve cognitive performance. They serve to keep your mind sharp, increase problem-solving abilities, and encourage creative thinking.

b. Stress Reduction: Engaging in a creative endeavour can be a kind of active relaxation. It allows you to focus on the current moment while taking a vacation from the demands of work, lowering tension, and generating a sense of serenity.

c. Emotional Release: Creative activities allow for self-expression and emotional release. They enable you to express your thoughts, emotions, and experiences in tangible ways, such as through art, writing, or music. This procedure can be cathartic and beneficial to mental clarity.

d. Mindfulness and Flow: When you are engaged in a creative endeavour, you reach a state of flow—complete absorption and focus. This state of flow is similar to mindfulness in that you are fully present in the moment, with a sense of timelessness and great focus.

Including Creative Activities in Your Daily Routine:

a. Identify Your Creative Outlet: Look for creative activities that interest you. Painting, writing, playing a musical instrument, dancing, photography, cooking, or any other kind of artistic expression could be considered. Experiment with various things to discover what offers you joy and sparks your creativity.

b. Make Time: Schedule time specifically for your creative endeavours. It can be as little as a few minutes per day or as long as several hours on weekends. Make this time a priority and consider it a vital element of your self-care regimen.

c. Make a Creative Area: Set aside an area in your house or business for your creative endeavours. Make it a welcoming and exciting setting that encourages your creativity. Surround yourself with tools, materials, and resources that will help you achieve your creative goals.

d. Accept Imperfection: Keep in mind that the goal of partaking in creative activities isn't just to create a masterpiece. It's about the journey of discovery, self-expression, and personal development. Accept your flaws and give yourself permission to experiment, learn, and grow through your artistic activities.

e. Seek Inspiration: Surround yourself with inspiring people. Visit art galleries, read books or blogs about your creative interests, listen to music that inspires you, or join creative communities to interact with others who share your interests. Taking inspiration from others can help you to be more creative.

Activities for Creativity:

a. Art: Painting, drawing, sculpting, or any other visual art form is acceptable. Experiment with various media, techniques, and styles. Allow yourself to express your emotions visually and creatively.

b. Writing and Journaling: Create a story, a poem, or a journal entry. Practise free writing, prompts, or storytelling. Writing helps you to express yourself, reflect on your experiences, and explore your creative side.

c. Music and Dance: Sing or dance to your favourite songs or play a musical instrument. Music and dancing can be effective forms of self-expression, emotional release, and brain stimulation.

d. Crafts and DIY Projects: Try your hand at woodworking, knitting, pottery, or any other craft that interests you. Making something with your own hands may be both mentally and emotionally rewarding.

e. Cooking and Baking: Experiment with new recipes, experiment with flavours, or create your own culinary creations. Cooking and baking can be considered artistic activities that engage your senses and inspire your imagination.

f. Photography and Filmmaking: Use a camera to explore the world. Capture memories, play with composition, and convey tales with your photos or videos. Photography and videography allow you to experience the world through new eyes and graphically express your ideas.

Conclusion:

Including creative activities in your self-care regimen is a great way to get some brain stimulation, self-expression, and emotional well-being. Find the creative activities that speak to you and create time for them in your hectic work life, whether it's through the visual arts, writing, music, dancing, crafts, cuisine, or photography. Accept the process, give yourself permission to experiment, and allow your creativity to blossom. Participating in creative endeavours will not only improve your mental clarity, but will also provide you with joy, fulfilment, and a revitalised sense of self.

Chapter 6

Rituals for Relational Connection

In our busy professional lives, it is essential not to overlook the significance of cultivating and sustaining meaningful relationships. Chapter 6 examines rituals that foster relational connection, allowing you to cultivate deeper relationships with loved ones, coworkers, and yourself. By prioritising relational health, you can improve your overall sense of satisfaction and equilibrium. Let's delve into the essential rituals for interpersonal bonding.

Establishing Effective Communication

Effective communication is the cornerstone of healthy relationships, as it facilitates comprehension, connection, and trust. This section explores rituals that foster authentic communication, an environment conducive to open dialogue, and fostering deeper connections.

1. Active Listening: This is a ritual that demonstrates genuine interest in the thoughts and feelings of others. Practise being completely present during conversations, free of distractions and interruptions. Maintain eye contact and provide both verbal and nonverbal cues to demonstrate that you are actively listening. While the other person is speaking, resist the urge to formulate a response and instead concentrate on understanding their perspective. By engaging in active listening, you create an environment in which individuals feel heard, valued, and understood, thereby strengthening the bond of trust, and nurturing deeper relationships.

Example: Imagine having a conversation with a coworker about their professional difficulties. Rather than waiting for your turn to speak or offering immediate solutions, actively attend to their issues, ask clarifying questions, and respond with understanding. This ritual encourages a deeper level of trust and understanding in your professional relationship by making them feel supported.

2. Compassionate Communication: It involves the use of language and tone that conveys empathy, respect, and comprehension. It requires cultivating self-awareness and selecting words that foster connection rather than hostility or judgement. Consider the impact of your words on others as you practise conveying yourself with authenticity. Aim to be sensitive to their emotions and perspectives, creating a space for communication that is safe and free of judgement. You cultivate a culture of understanding, empathy, and collaboration by incorporating compassionate communication into your interactions.

Example: When providing feedback on a colleague's work in a team meeting, use compassionate communication to convey your observations and suggestions. Rather than criticising their abilities, focus on specific behaviours or areas for improvement. Frame your feedback in a supportive and constructive manner, highlighting the contribution's value. This ritual promotes open communication and strengthens the team's working relationships.

3. Setting Communication Boundaries: In today's chaotic digital world, it is essential to establish communication boundaries to maintain a healthy balance between personal and professional relationships. Establish distinct guidelines and expectations regarding the time and manner of your communication. Define specific times for work-related communications, such as email and phone calls, and establish boundaries to safeguard your personal time and well-being. By establishing limits on communication, you make room for self-care, concentration, and uninterrupted connections with loved ones.

Example: Determine specific time periods throughout the day for focused work and minimise interruptions. Communicate these limitations to your coworkers and indicate your availability for meetings or conversations. Establish designated periods during which you disconnect from work-related communication in order to prioritise personal time with family or activities that provide mental and emotional recharging. This ritual promotes a healthy work-life balance and ensures that your relationships receive the time and attention they deserve.

Time and Connections

Developing strong and meaningful relationships requires deliberate effort and time spent together. This section examines rituals that emphasise spending quality time with loved ones, coworkers, and oneself, thereby nurturing deeper connections and a sense of belonging.

1. Weekly Family Rituals: These provide an opportunity for familial bonding, shared experiences, and the strengthening of familial ties. Establish weekly family traditions or activities, such as a family game night, a regular family meal, or a weekend excursion. These rituals provide opportunities for amusement, meaningful discourse, and the cultivation of relationships. The family's dedication to these rituals fosters a sense of unity, trust, and support.

Example: Sunday afternoons should be designated as family excursion time. Plan activities that will appeal to everyone, such as picnics, treks, and visits to local attractions. Each member of the family should take shifts selecting the activity, so that everyone feels included and valued. This ritual strengthens family ties and creates memories to be cherished.

2. Date Nights or Hangouts with Friends: Nurturing romantic relationships and friendships requires time set aside for connection and shared experiences. Plan regular date nights with your companion and hangouts with your closest friends to foster deeper relationships outside of your daily routine. Use this time to engage in enjoyable activities, have meaningful conversations, and create memories that will last a lifetime. These rituals strengthen emotional connections, revitalise relationships, and provide a channel for support and comprehension.

Example: Set aside one evening every other week for an engagement with your significant other. Plan activities such as dining out, viewing a movie, or participating in a common hobby. Alternately, plan monthly get-togethers with your friends where you can catch up, investigate new places, or participate in activities that bring you joy. These rituals prioritise relationship maintenance and create a space for hilarity, openness, and connection.

3. Personal Retreats: In the midst of hectic professional situations, it is essential to schedule time for personal retreats in order to reconnect with oneself. These retreats provide the opportunity to engage in activities that bring you happiness, introspection, and rejuvenation. Personal retreats provide an opportunity for self-reflection, introspection, and self-connection, whether it's a day or weekend escape or a designated time for self-care rituals.

Example: Plan a weekend retreat at a tranquil retreat centre or reserve a cottage in the woods. Engage in soul-nourishing activities, such as yoga, meditation, journaling, or simply savouring solitude in a natural setting, during this time. Allow yourself the space to recharge and reconnect with your inner self by using this time to reflect on your personal goals, ambitions, and aspirations. These retreats encourage self-care, self-discovery, and a renewed sense of purpose.

Gratitude Expressions and Kindness Acts

Not only do expressing gratitude and performing acts of compassion benefit others, but they also foster relational connection and well-being. This section discusses rituals that encourage gratitude and compassion in your relationships.

1. Gratitude Practises: The cultivation of a daily gratitude practise can have a significant impact on your relationships. Every day, take a moment to express gratitude to the individuals in your life. Keep a gratitude journal in which you list specific items for which you are thankful, express your gratitude in conversation, or write thank-you notes. By practising gratitude, you cultivate a positive and appreciative attitude, which strengthens relational ties and increases overall relationship satisfaction.

Example: Before going to bed each night, note down three things you appreciate about your spouse or a close friend. Share with your loved one the specific qualities, actions, or moments for which you are grateful. This ritual fosters a sense of appreciation, strengthens emotional bonds, and fortifies the bond of gratitude between you.

2. Random Acts of Kindness: Random acts of kindness are a gorgeous way to demonstrate concern and support for others. Consider opportunities to be kind throughout the day, such as assisting a coworker with a task, lending an ear to a friend in need, or conducting a small act of service for a member of your family. These acts of generosity illustrate your thoughtfulness, compassion, and willingness to assist others, nurturing a sense of connection and reciprocity in your relationships.

Example: Surprise a coworker with their favourite coffee or treat, write an encouraging note to a friend, or offer to assist a family member with a difficult task. These small acts of kindness have a profound effect, demonstrating your concern and fostering your relationships.

3. Celebrating Milestones and Accomplishments: Taking the time to recognise and celebrate the milestones and accomplishments of your loved ones and coworkers is a crucial ritual for fostering relational connection. Whether it's a promotion, a commencement, or a personal achievement, recognising and congratulating their success demonstrates your support and validation. Celebrating milestones strengthens your relationship and demonstrates that you care about their happiness and well-being.

Example: To honour a colleague's professional accomplishment, you could host a modest gathering or send a gift of congratulations. Plan a special dinner or excursion to celebrate a loved one's personal achievement. Take the time to express your pride and gratitude for their hard work and to jointly celebrate their success. This ritual fosters a sense of community, elevates happiness, and strengthens your relationships.

Conclusion:

The sixth chapter focuses on rituals for relational connection, emphasising the importance of genuine communication, quality time spent together, expressing gratitude, and engaging in acts of charity. By incorporating these rituals into your routine of self-care, you nurture and deepen your relationships, nurturing a sense of belonging, support, and fulfilment in your hectic professional life. Keep in mind that establishing and maintaining strong relationships requires effort, consistency, and a genuine desire to connect. Embrace these rituals and witness your relationships flourish, bringing you happiness, understanding, and deep connections.

Chapter 7

Rituals for Soulful Renewal

Even if you have a busy schedule and a demanding job, it's important to make soul renewal a top priority. This chapter talks about rituals that feed your inner self, give you time to think and relax, and help you get in touch with your deeper goals and hobbies. By adding these habits to your self-care routine, you make room for soulful renewal and get in touch with what really makes you happy and satisfied.

Connecting with Nature

Nature has a big effect on our health and happiness because it gives us ideas, peace, and a sense of belonging to something bigger than ourselves. This part goes into detail about rituals that help you connect deeply with nature and feel its healing and restoring power.

1. Regular Walks: Take regular walks in nature. This is a great way to enjoy the beauty of the world around you. Explore your neighbourhood parks, woods, or beaches and pay attention to the sights, sounds, and smells around you. Take slow, thoughtful steps that let you be fully in the moment and aware of the beauty of nature. These walks help you relax, cut down on stress, and improve your overall well-being.

Example: Set aside one evening a week to go for a walk in nature. Leave your electronics behind and take a slow walk through a nearby park. Look at the bright colours of the flowers, listen to the birds singing, or hear the leaves rustling. Let yourself get completely lost in the beauty of nature. This will refresh your soul and help you feel calm.

2. Gardening: When you garden, you can get in touch with the land and help plants grow. Taking care of plants, whether you have a small herb garden inside or a big oasis in your backyard, can be a relaxing and soul-enriching routine. Get your hands dirty, plant seeds, water and care for your plants, and watch the beauty of nature develop before your eyes. Gardening helps people pay attention, be patient, and feel responsible for the world.

Example: Set aside a part of your backyard or use potted plants to make a small garden inside. Take care of your yard by watering the plants, pulling out weeds, and watching them grow. As you spend time with nature and watch your plants grow and change, you'll feel joy, satisfaction, and a greater connection to the natural world.

3. Sunrise or Sunset Rituals: Seeing the sunrise or sunset can be very soul-nourishing. Seeing the sky's colours change and the quiet change from day to night is awe-inspiring and relaxing. Make it a habit to wake up early or find a quiet place to watch the sunset, and be fully present during these beautiful times. Think about the beauty of nature, say thank you, or do a few minutes of deep breathing or meditation.

Example: Set your alarm for early in the morning and find a quiet place to watch the sunrise. Find a relaxed spot, watch the sky get lighter, and take a few moments to think about how beautiful it is that the world is waking up. You could also find a quiet place to watch the sky change colours as the sun goes down and let the peace of the moment wash over you. These habits connect you to the natural rhythms of the day and fill your soul with a sense of renewal and joy.

Engaging in Soulful Practises

To take care of your soul, you have to do more than just take care of your body. You have to do things that are in line with your values, passions, and personal growth. This part talks about rituals that can help you get in touch with your inner wisdom, spark your creativity, and do things that make you happy and feel fulfilled.

1. Meditation and Mindfulness: Using meditation and adding daily mindfulness practises can give you a deep feeling of soulful renewal. Take some time to sit still, focus on your breath, and develop a sense of being present and aware. Let your mind settle, watch your thoughts without judging them, and make room for peace and clarity inside yourself. Meditation and mindfulness routines help you think about yourself, lower stress, and improve your overall health.

Example: Set aside a certain time each day for meditation and practising awareness Find somewhere quiet to sit and focus on your breath. Let your thoughts come and go. When they do, gently bring your mind back to the present. Start with just a few minutes and eventually add more time as you get better. These practises give your soul a safe place and help you become more self-aware.

2. Using Creative Outlets: When you do creative things, you can get in touch with your inner interests and show who you are. Whether it's painting, writing, playing music, or making something, creative routines are a way to express yourself, learn more about yourself, and grow as a person. Give yourself permission to try new things, accept your flaws, and express your talent without judgement or expectations.

Example: Set aside a certain amount of time each week for a creative project that you enjoy. It could be painting in your art studio, writing in a notebook, playing an instrument, or doing anything else that makes you feel creative and happy. Let yourself get completely lost in the process and enjoy the times of inspiration and the satisfaction of making something from the heart. These habits help you be more creative, learn more about yourself, and feel like your life is complete.

3. Soulful Reading: Reading and thinking about books that inspire, challenge, and uplift your spirit is a strong way to renew your soul. Choose books that match your hobbies, help you grow as a person, or help you explore your spirituality. Spend time getting lost in the words and letting the knowledge and insights sink into your soul. Think about the messages, write down your thoughts and feelings in a book, and use the lessons in your life.

Example: Make a list of books that fit with what your mind wants to read. Set aside time each week to read these books, whether it's in the morning, at lunch, or before you go to sleep. As you read, stop to think about the parts that speak to you, write down your thoughts, and let the knowledge feed your soul. These practises can help you grow, broaden your view of the world, and learn more about yourself and the world.

Practising Mindful Self-Reflection

Soul restoration requires thinking about yourself, being aware of yourself, and having a deep knowledge of your values and wants. This part talks about rituals that help you connect with your inner self and make sure your actions are in line with what you really want.

1. Solitude and Silence: Carving out moments of solitude and silence is essential for soulful renewal. Find a place where you can be alone with your thoughts and unbothered by anything outside of yourself. Take advantage of the quiet and the chance to listen to your inner voice, notice your feelings, and get clear on your ideas and desires. Rituals of solitude and silence can be a safe place for self-reflection, self-discovery, and getting in touch with your inner self.

Example: Set aside a certain amount of time each day for peace and quiet. Find a comfortable place where you can be alone, like a cosy part of your home or a quiet spot in nature. Close your eyes, turn off your electronics, and enjoy the quiet. Let your thoughts come up without judging them, watch them, and try to feel calm inside. These rituals are good for self-reflection because they give you a chance to connect with your real self and get clear in the middle of a busy life.

2. Journaling for Self-Exploration: Journaling is a powerful tool for self-reflection and self-expression. By writing down your ideas and feelings, you give yourself a chance to think about yourself, learn more about yourself, and grow as a person. Write down your thoughts, dreams, and goals, and give yourself permission to explore your inner world.

Example: Set aside time every day to write in your journal, whether it's in the morning to set goals for the day or in the evening to think about what you've done. Write openly, without judging yourself or putting a stop to your ideas. Explore your emotions, dreams, and problems to learn more about your hopes, fears, and goals. These rituals give you a safe place to express yourself and learn more about yourself. They help you get to know yourself better and build a soulful relationship.

3. Gratitude Practise: Having a gratitude practise helps you stop thinking about what you don't have and start thinking about what you do have. This ritual helps you have a good attitude, be grateful for the moment you're in, and feel more connected to the blessings and chances around you. Take time every day to think about the big and small things you're grateful for and say thank you.

Example: Include a daily practise of thanksgiving in your daily life. Set aside a few minutes each day, maybe in the morning or before bed, to write down three things you are thankful for. Think about the people, events, or small things that make you happy and tell them how much you appreciate them. Gratitude practises can change the way you see things, make you more positive, and give your soul a sense of contentment and plenty.

Engaging in Hobbies and Activities That Bring Joy

In the busy world of professionals, it's easy to forget about the things that make us happy and excited. But it's important to have hobbies and activities that spark our interests if we want to feel fulfilled and connected to our souls. This section talks about how important it is to take part in hobbies and activities that make you happy and gives you ways to add them to your self-care practise.

1. Rediscovering Childhood Hobbies: Do you remember the things you did as a child that gave you a lot of joy and excitement? Whether it was painting, playing an instrument, or doing a certain sport, going back to your old hobbies can bring back your sense of joy and help you connect with your inner kid. Give yourself time to do these things and let yourself fully enjoy the happiness they bring.

If you loved painting as a child, get some art supplies and make a place in your home where you can paint. Set aside time regularly to get lost in the colours and textures, which will help your imagination flow. Getting back into old hobbies from your childhood is not only fun, but also gives you a feeling of nostalgia and a closer connection to your true self.

2. Try New Hobbies and Interests: Life has a lot of different things you can do, and you may have hobbies or interests that are just waiting to be found. Trying new things not only makes you feel excited but also helps you grow and learn about yourself. Be willing to try new things, like learning to play an instrument, getting better at shooting, or signing up for a dance class. Learning and trying out new hobbies can be fun and help you see more of the world.

Example: Look into classes, workshops, or clubs in your area that offer things that interest you. Join a book club, take up martial arts, or sign up for a cooking class. Get out of your comfort zone and take advantage of the chance to learn and do things that interest you. Trying out new hobbies makes you feel like you're starting over and gives you a new lease on life.

3. Play and Recreation: This should be a priority: As adults, we often forget how important play and leisure are to our lives. Taking part in things just for fun and enjoyment can have a big effect on our health and happiness. Whether it's through sports, board games, or trips in the great outdoors, making playtime a priority helps us relax, relieve stress, and feel pure joy.

Example: Set aside time on a daily basis to do fun things that make you happy. Set up a game night with your friends or coworkers, go hiking with your family, or join a recreational sports club. When you make play and relaxation a priority, you not only get rid of stress, but you also feel joy, spontaneity, and childlike wonder again.

4. Be Creative: Creativity is a way to show yourself and find out what you're good at and what you're passionate about. Whether you paint, write, sing, or do something else creative, giving your creativity time to grow gives you a deep feeling of fulfilment and soulful connection.

Example: Set aside regular time for the artistic activity you want to do. Set up a place in your home where you can write, a corner where you can paint, or a room where you can practise music. Make it a habit to do creative things that let you express yourself easily and use your special skills. Having creative outlets gives you a sense of meaning and makes you feel like your life is complete.

By getting back into old hobbies, trying out new ones, making play and recreation a priority, and finding ways to be creative, you can fill your life with times of pure joy and fulfilment. Make a promise to yourself to do these things as part of your self-care practise and give yourself the gift of true happiness and a soul-renewing experience. Take advantage of the power of hobbies and activities that make you happy, and watch as they make your busy work life better.

Conclusion:

In Chapter 7, Rituals for Meaningful Renewal, the author talks about how important it is to connect with nature, do meaningful things, and think about yourself with care. These rituals give you chances to connect with your inner purpose, spark your creativity, and get in touch with what really makes you happy and fulfilled. By adding these self-care rituals to your busy work life, you can feed your soul, find inner peace, and live a more purposeful and fulfilling life. Accept these rituals and let them lead you on a journey to renew your soul.

Chapter 8

Cultivating Self-Compassion and Love

It is easy to neglect the significance of self-compassion and self-love in the demanding and chaotic world of busy professionals. Nonetheless, these characteristics are fundamental to our overall health, resilience, and ability to navigate the challenges we face. This chapter examines the transformative force of self-compassion and self-love and offers daily rituals and strategies for strengthening them.

Self-Compassion

1. Recognising the Importance of Self-Compassion:

Self-compassion is one of the most important parts of taking care of yourself and building a good relationship with yourself. It means being kind, understanding, and accepting of ourselves, especially when things are hard or when we judge ourselves. The first step to putting self-compassion into our lives is to understand what it means.

Example: Imagine a time when you did something wrong or didn't get the result you wanted. Self-compassion is a better way to handle the problem than self-criticism. Recognise that everyone makes mistakes and that this is a chance to learn and grow. Give yourself kindness and understanding, and remember that you are a person like everyone else and deserve sympathy just like they do.

2. Embracing Self-Acceptance: Self-acceptance depends on being able to accept yourself. It means accepting ourselves as we are, with all of our skills, weaknesses, flaws, and mistakes. When we accept ourselves as we are, we don't have to keep looking for support or approval from other people.

Example: Take a moment to think about the parts of yourself that you tend to criticise or judge. Accept these parts of yourself and be kind to yourself. Recognise that everyone has skills and flaws that are unique to them. It's these things that make us all special. When we accept ourselves, we can build a deep sense of self-worth and be true to ourselves.

3. Developing Self-Kindness: Kindness towards yourself is a key part of self-compassion. It means being kind, gentle, and understanding towards ourselves. Instead of being mean to ourselves or criticising ourselves, self-kindness means treating ourselves with the same love and care we would give to a close friend or loved one.

Example: Listen to what you say to yourself. Notice when you're being hard on yourself and choose to treat yourself with kindness. When you talk to yourself, use words that are kind and helpful. Instead of judging yourself, say something kind and understanding. Take care of yourself like you would a close friend who needs help.

4. Embracing Common Humanity: Self-compassion means understanding that pain, problems, and flaws are all parts of being human. It means knowing that we are not alone in our problems and that other people go through the same things. Accepting that we are all humans makes us feel connected to and care about ourselves and other people.

Example: Think about a challenge you are having right now. Know that other people have or are going through similar problems. Remind yourself that hard times and failures are a normal part of life. By focusing on what we all have in common, we can feel more empathy and kindness, both for ourselves and for other people.

Understanding self-compassion is a key step towards building a good relationship with ourselves. By recognising the value of self-compassion, embracing self-acceptance, practising self-kindness, and embracing our shared humanity, we lay the groundwork for a more compassionate and nurturing self-care practise. By putting these ideas into practise, we can deal with our own problems and flaws with kindness, understanding, and acceptance. This helps us be healthier and more resilient as busy workers.

Nurturing Self-Love

1. Practising Self-Care as an Act of Love: When we love ourselves, we put our own needs first and take care of our bodies, minds, and spirits. It affirms our worthiness of receiving affection, consideration, and care. Taking care of oneself is a vital act of self-love and self-respect.

Example: You may develop your own self-care programme that targets all elements of your health. Taking a warm bath, reading a book, practising yoga, or going for a walk in the park are all examples of activities that could fall into this category. Do things that make you feel good on all levels, and make self-care an integral part of your routine.

2. Cultivating Positive Self-Talk: The way we talk about ourselves has a big impact on our level of self-love. To practise positive self-talk, one must first recognise destructive thought patterns and then work to replace them with more constructive, encouraging internal monologue. Self-love and confidence can be cultivated by replacing negative self-talk with a more constructive story.

Example: Think about the things you believe to be true about yourself. Stop and question your negative or self-deprecating ideas when you notice yourself thinking them. Swap them out for more upbeat and encouraging language. Affirm to yourself every day that you are worthy of love and happiness, that you accept yourself flaws and all, and that you deserve the best life has to offer.

3. Embracing Self-Compassion in Mistakes and Setbacks: To truly love oneself is to accept oneself completely, flaws and all. It implies accepting the fact that we are fallible humans and will make mistakes. Adopting an attitude of self-compassion rather than harsh self-criticism might help us get past setbacks and move forward with our lives.

Example: You should treat yourself nicely whenever you experience adversity or make mistakes in life. Keep in mind that failure is normal and can be used as a learning experience. Just as you would comfort and encourage a loved one going through a similar situation, show yourself care and empathy. Accept your mistakes as chances to learn and get better.

4. Setting Limits and Saying No: Respecting one's own needs and limits is an important part of cultivating self-love. To practise this means to accept that it is acceptable to decline requests or demands from others when doing so would be detrimental to one's own well-being or values. By establishing limits, we may safeguard our mental and emotional well-being and put ourselves first.

Example: Saying "no" when you need to can help you practise setting limits. Evaluate your responsibilities and resolve to fulfil only those that are in line with your ideals and best for your happiness. Focus on what makes you happy and fulfilled, and learn to say "no" to what drains your energy or crosses your boundaries. Keep in mind that setting boundaries and saying "no" is a kind of self-care.

As hardworking professionals, our health and happiness depend on our ability to take time for ourselves and practise self-love. We can learn to love, accept, and respect ourselves deeply by treating self-care as an act of love, engaging in positive self-talk, embracing self-compassion in mistakes and setbacks, and establishing healthy boundaries. By engaging in these routines, we strengthen our capacity for resilience and improve our capacity to focus on our own well-being. Self-love is a practise that must be maintained over the course of a lifetime if we are to enjoy more satisfying and purposeful personal and professional lives.

Building Resilience and Self-Compassion

1. Embracing Imperfection and Self-Compassion: Recognising and accepting our flaws and failures with self-compassion is essential to developing resilience. This means giving up the illusion that we can ever be perfect and instead embracing our humanity despite our many flaws. Resilience and composure in the face of adversity can be developed through the practise of self-compassion.

Example: Consider times when you had to overcome obstacles or correct your own faults as an illustration. Instead of beating yourself up, try being kind to yourself. Try to keep in mind that failure and error are common occurrences. Recognise your human frailties and be kind to yourself instead of constantly berating yourself.

2. Developing a Growth Mindset: A growth mindset is the conviction that one's talents and IQ may be enhanced through focused study and practise. When we adopt a growth mindset, we train ourselves to be more resilient and to see setbacks as openings for learning and development. This frame of mind equips us to deal with challenges in a constructive and hopeful manner.

Example: Apply a growth attitude, for instance, when dealing with a challenging assignment or a setback. Consider this a chance to expand your horizons rather than a sign of your own inadequacies. Challenges are opportunities to grow as a person and acquire valuable experience and insight.

3. Practising Self-Care During Times of Stress: Self-care should be a top priority at all times, but it is especially important for building resilience and self-compassion during times of stress and adversity. Taking care of one's physical, emotional, and mental health is critical in avoiding burnout and keeping one's resilience levels up. Taking care of yourself can help you feel more resilient in stressful situations and give you the energy boost you need to get through them.

Example: Determine what you enjoy doing to unwind and re-energise. Doing something you enjoy, going outside, meditating, or leaning on friends and family are all good examples of this. Maintaining your health and happiness in the face of a hectic work schedule requires incorporating self-care rituals into your everyday life.

4. Establishing Positive Relationships: The road to resiliency and self-compassion is shared. Building resilient ties and having someone you can lean on emotionally in times of need is essential. Your ability to recover from adversity can be greatly improved by surrounding yourself with supportive, encouraging people.

Example: Create a community of people who understand and can support you, such as friends, family, or coworkers. Find someone with whom you can be honest about your struggles, triumphs, and feelings. Talk to people, learn from them, and help others around you. Having a strong social network might help you feel more connected to others and boost your ability to bounce back from adversity.

Conclusion:

Self-compassion and self-love are discussed in depth in Chapter 8 as a means of personal transformation. You can develop a deep sense of love and compassion for yourself by understanding how important self-compassion is, accepting self-acceptance, fostering self-love through self-care and positive self-talk, and building resilience through embracing imperfection and forgiving yourself.

These habits will not only help you feel better in general, but also equip you with the strength, resiliency, and self-love you need to handle the stresses of a demanding career.

Adopting these practises can help you make self-care and self-love your guiding principles on the path to self-improvement.

"Self-care is the key to unlocking your full potential."

Chapter 9

Rituals for Time Management and Productivity

In a world filled with constant demands and limited hours in a day, it's crucial for busy professionals to optimise their time so they can accomplish their goals efficiently. This chapter gives you useful routines and tips that will help you take charge of your schedule, set priorities, and find a good balance between work and your personal life. Get ready to change the way you handle your time and find out how productive you can really be. Let's dive in!

Setting Priorities and Time Blocking

You need to be able to handle your time well in order to be as productive as possible and keep a good work-life balance. By making a list of goals and using time-blocking methods, you can improve your ability to concentrate, cut down on distractions, and make the most of your time.

1. Knowing Priorities and Goals: Start by making a list of your top responsibilities and short-term and long-term goals. This will help you figure out how to best spend your time and energy. Think about the jobs and projects that help you reach your goals and improve your general success and happiness.

Example: Make a list of the things you have to do and the goals you want to reach. Consider how critical and time-sensitive they are. Find the jobs that will help you grow the most professionally and personally. By knowing what your goals are, you can use your time and resources in the best way.

2. Implementing Time Blocking: Time blocking is a strong method in which you schedule different jobs or activities for specific blocks of time. By giving specific jobs their own time slots, you can cut down on distractions and improve your ability to focus and get things done. It gives you a sense of order and lets you work quickly and well.

Example: Break up your job into chunks of time that you can use for different tasks. For example, set aside a certain amount of time in the morning for high-priority chores that take a lot of focus. Set aside another time slot for talks and group projects. Make sure you take breaks and take care of yourself to keep your energy up and avoid burning out.

3. Controlling External and Internal Distractions: Find and deal with both external and internal things that get in the way of your work. External distractions include phone messages, email alerts, or noisy surroundings. Internal distractions can include doing too many things at once, talking badly to yourself, or not knowing what your top goals are. By cutting down on these distractions, you can stay on task and get things done more quickly.

Example: Turn off distracting alerts when you need to work. Set times to check texts and messages instead of responding to them all the time. Use methods for being aware to calm the mind and stop it from wandering. Make a specific place to work that helps you stay on task and reduces distractions.

Strategies for Getting Things Done

Organising tasks is important for staying productive and avoiding being too busy. By using good methods for managing your tasks, you can make your work run more smoothly, stay organised, and make sure that important tasks are done on time.

1. Setting Priorities and Organising tasks: Set jobs in order of importance, urgency, and dates. Break up big jobs into smaller tasks that are easier to handle. To keep track of your chores and goals, use tools like to-do lists or digital apps. Set up your jobs in a way that helps you stay focused and fits with your goals.

Example: At the start of each day, look over your list of chores and figure out which ones are the most important. Sort them by how urgent and important they are. Break down big jobs into steps that can be done. To keep track of and organise your work well, use tools like project management software or productivity apps.

2. Employing Time-Effective Techniques: Adopt time-saving methods to make yourself more efficient and productive. Some of these methods are the Pomodoro Technique and the Eisenhower Matrix. With the Pomodoro Technique, you work in short, focused bursts that are followed by short breaks. Try out different ways to find the ones that work best for you.

Example: Set a timer for 25 minutes of focused work, then take a 5-minute break. This is the Pomodoro Technique. Repeat this cycle three or four times, then take a longer break. Use the Eisenhower Matrix to divide tasks into four groups: tasks that are urgent and important, tasks that are important but not urgent, tasks that are urgent but not important, and tasks that are neither urgent nor important. First, you should work on the jobs in the first two quadrants.

3. Delegating and Outsourcing: Know when chores can be given to other people or "outsourced." Giving away jobs that don't need your direct care gives you time for more important tasks. You can also improve productivity by giving jobs to professionals or using automation tools. This will let you focus on what you do best.

Example: Find out what tasks your coworkers or team members are capable of performing well. Give those jobs to someone else, and make sure they know what is expected of them. Think about hiring freelancers or specialised companies to do things like office work, graphic design, or writing content. Use apps or tools to automate jobs that you do often.

Creating Rituals for Work-Life Integration

Integrating your work and home life means finding a good mix between the two. By making rituals that help you balance work and life, you can set limits, improve your health, and make sure that both parts of your life get enough care.

1. Establishing Boundaries and Work-Life Balance:

Set clear limits between work and personal life to avoid burnout and encourage a healthy balance between work and personal life. Set clear work hours and let your coworkers and clients know about them. Make routines that show the change from work to personal time, like turning off your computer or doing something relaxing.

Example: Figure out your best working hours and tell your coworkers and clients about them. Don't check texts or messages connected to work outside of these times. Make a routine for the end of the workday, like going for a walk or doing a sport, to show that it's time to stop working and spend time on yourself.

2. Engaging in Self-Care Rituals:

Include self-care practises in your daily schedule to put your health and happiness first. Some of these routines can be things like working out, meditating, reading, or spending time with people you care about. Make self-care an important part of your plan. This will improve your general health and give you more energy.

Example: Set aside specific times in your plan to do things for yourself. Whether it's an exercise in the morning, a meditation break in the middle of the day, or a walk with your family in the evening, do things for yourself that give you physical, emotional, and mental energy.

3. Maximising Technology for Efficiency:

Use technology to help you balance your work and personal life. Use productivity apps, communication tools, and project management software to simplify your work, make it easier to work together, and spend less time on routine tasks. Choose tools that meet your needs and help you get your work done more quickly.

Example: Look into productivity apps that can help you keep track of your chores, set notes, and monitor your progress. Use tools for project management to work well with your team and keep everyone up-to-date on project changes. Use tools for conversation that let you talk clearly and quickly, so you don't have to send and receive so many emails.

Conclusion:

Chapter 9 was about routines that help you handle your time and get things done. These are important for busy professionals who are trying to balance their work and home lives. By setting goals and using time blocks, you can improve your ability to focus and get things done. With good methods for managing tasks, you can stay organised and meet goals easily. By making work-life routines, you can be sure to keep your limits, put self-care first, and get the most out of technology. By making these habits a part of your daily life, you can build a satisfying and well-balanced career path while taking care of your overall wellness.

"Your well-being is non-negotiable."

Chapter 10

Personal Growth and Development

In this world of constant change, it's important to invest in your own growth if you want to be happy and successful. Through a set of powerful practises, we want to give you the tools and methods you need to keep learning, set goals that matter, and accept change. Get ready to find your real potential and start a journey of self-discovery and self-improvement that will change your life.

Continuing Education and Skill Development

Continuing education and acquiring new skills are important for both personal and professional growth. By committing to life-long learning and gaining new knowledge and skills, you can expand your views, adapt to changing environments, and open up new possibilities for personal and professional growth.

1. Pursuing Formal Education and Training:

Think about signing up for classes, workshops, or certification programmes that match your hobbies and career goals. Formal education gives you organised ways to learn and lets you learn more about and become an expert in certain areas. It can be done through regular schools, online venues, or professional groups.

Example: Look into training programmes that are related to your job or interests. Look for classes or certifications in those areas at respectable schools or online sites. Before making a choice, you should think about how much time, money, and perks each programme requires.

2. Engaging in Continuous Learning:

Adopt a "growth mindset" and make it a habit to keep learning. Read books, listen to podcasts, and follow thought leaders in your field to stay up-to-date on what's going on in your field. You can learn from experts and grow your business network by going to workshops, webinars, and classes.

Example: Set aside time each week for things that help you learn. Make a list of books and articles that are about your field or will help you grow as a person. Check out podcasts or TED Talks that can help you learn something new. Join online groups or communities to meet people who share your interests and take part in talks.

3. Developing New Skills:

Find skills that are in demand or that add to what you already know. Spend time learning and improving these skills to make yourself more valuable in the workplace. These skills could be technical, like coding or analysing data, or soft, like speaking, leading, or fixing problems.

Example: Find out what skills are in high demand in your field or are needed to move up in your job. Find ways that you can get better or learn new skills. Use online sites that teach these skills through classes or guides. Practise often and look for ways to use the new skills you've learned in the real world.

Setting Personal Goals for Growth

Setting goals for yourself is an important part of growing as a person. By setting clear goals and making plans for how to reach them, you can map out a road to self-improvement, boost your self-confidence, and feel a sense of accomplishment as you reach your goals.

1. Thinking About Personal Goals:

Take some time to think about your personal and business goals. Find out where you want to improve, what problems you want to solve, and what goals you want to reach. When making personal goals, you should think about your ideals, passions, and long-term goals.

Example: Take time to think about your goals and write them down in a book. Ask yourself things like, "What do I want to accomplish in the next 12 months?" What do I want to learn or get better at? How can I picture my best future? Use these thoughts as a guide for setting goals.

2. Setting SMART Goals:

Use the SMART structure to set goals that matter and can be reached. SMART stands for Specific, Measurable, Achievable, Relevant, and Time-bound. When you set SMART goals, you make sure that your goals are clear, measurable, achievable, in line with your values, and have a clear date.

Example: Instead of saying, "I want to improve my communication skills," make your goal SMART by stating what you want to happen. For example, you could say, "I want to finish a public speaking course in the next three months to improve my presentation skills and confidence in front of an audience."

3. Creating Action Plans:

After you've set your goals, break them down into steps you can take to reach them. Make detailed action plans that list the jobs, tools, and time frames you'll need to reach each goal. Review and change your action plans often to make sure you stay on track and make progress towards your goals.

Example: Break up your goals into smaller jobs or steps. Find out what tools or help you need to complete each job. Make a schedule with due dates for each major step. Check your work often and make changes when you need to.

Embracing Change and Expanding Comfort Zones

Getting better and growing as a person often means getting out of your comfort zone and being open to change. By pushing yourself, taking measured risks, and welcoming new experiences, you can increase your skills, build your confidence, and open up new ways to grow.

1. Embracing Discomfort:

Know that you grow as a person when you go outside of your comfort zone. Accept that being uncomfortable is a sign of growth and learning. Be ready to take on new tasks and deal with situations that may seem strange or scary at first.

Example: Do things that push you to the limits of what you can do. Volunteer for projects at work that will help you learn new skills or give you a chance to lead. Find ways to get out of your normal pattern and do things that will give you new views and experiences.

2. Taking Calculated Risks:

Think about the risks and benefits of getting out of your comfort zone. Taking risks means being open to the unknown, but taking measured risks can lead to personal growth and new chances. Think about what could happen, weigh the pros and cons, and then make a choice.

Example: Consider looking for a new job, starting a side business, or taking on a challenging leadership position. Think about the risks and benefits, ask mentors or trusted coworkers for help, and make choices that are in line with your long-term goals.

3. Learning from Failure and Adaptation:

Failure is a common part of growing up. Accept mistakes as chances to learn and draw lessons from them. Change your method, improve your plans, and keep going even when things don't go as planned. Use losing as a way to improve yourself and become stronger.

Example: When you fail or have a loss, think about what you've learned and where you can make changes. Change your plans or ask your teachers or peers for comments. Adopt a "growth mindset" and see mistakes as chances to learn and improve.

Conclusion:

In Chapter 10, we looked at routines for personal growth and development. We learned how important it is to keep learning, set goals, and be open to change. By always learning new things, getting new skills, and staying up-to-date in your area, you can increase your professional value. Setting goals for yourself gives you direction and the desire to improve yourself. Accepting pain, taking measured risks, and learning from mistakes help you grow and open up new opportunities. By adding these routines to your daily life, you can start a journey of personal growth and reach your full potential, both personally and professionally.

"You are worthy of rest, relaxation, and rejuvenation."

Chapter 11

Balancing Work and Leisure

In our hectic and chaotic world, it's important to find a good mix between work and play for your general health and to live a full life. In this chapter, we look into routines and methods for striking a balance between work and personal life, which enables even the busiest professionals to make time for relaxation, personal development, and satisfaction.

Understanding the Importance of Work-Life Balance

1. The Impact of Imbalance:

When work is more important than other things in life, it can lead to burnout, more stress, and troubled relationships. If you don't take care of your hobbies and interests, it can make you feel less fulfilled and hurt your general health.

Example: Imagine a person who always works long hours and misses out on time with family and friends because of it. Over time, this can lead to a sense of being alone, broken relationships, and unhappiness, even if the person is successful at work.

2. Benefits of Work-Life Balance:

Having a good mix between work and life has many perks. It improves people's physical and mental health, makes them more productive and focused, makes their relationships stronger, and lets them follow their own hobbies and interests.

Example: Think about a person who has a good mix between work and personal life. They set aside time for work-related tasks as well as things like spending valuable time with loved ones, doing hobbies, and taking care of their physical and mental health. This balanced method helps people feel better, happier, and more fulfilled in general.

Strategies for Achieving Work-Life Balance
1. Establishing Boundaries:

To find a good mix between work and personal life, you must set clear limits between the two. Setting work hours and non-negotiable personal time and letting coworkers and loved ones know about these limits, can help create a sense of separation and give you time to focus on your own needs and interests.

Example: Set specific work hours and make a promise to stick to them. Tell your coworkers and clients about these limits and stress how important personal time is outside of work. Use tools like email autoresponders to let people know when you're available when you're not at work.

2. Prioritising Self-Care:

Self-care is an important part of balancing work and life. Putting self-care tasks like exercise, rest, and hobbies at the top of your list can help you recharge and feel better overall.

Example: Set aside regular time to do things for yourself, like exercise, meditation, or your hobbies and interests. Self-care should be something you can't skip, so put it on your plan just like you would any other important task.

3. Effective Time Management:

Getting a good mix between work and life means making good use of your time. By putting chores in order of importance, making realistic goals, and using time management methods, you can get more done and have more time for fun and personal things.

Example: Use time management methods like the Pomodoro Technique, in which you work in short, focused bursts and then take short breaks. Set priorities for tasks based on how important they are and when they need to be done. When you can, share or outsource tasks to free up time for things you want to do outside of work.

4. Delegation and Outsourcing:

Realise that you don't have to do everything yourself. When you delegate tasks at work and outsource some of your personal chores, you can reduce stress and have more time for fun and self-care.

Example: Tasks can be assigned to coworkers or team members who have the skills and time to do them. Hire someone else to do your housework or think about getting virtual help for your office work. By giving up some of your tasks, you can make more time for fun and personal things.

Fostering meaningful leisure activities

1. Pursuing Hobbies and Interests:

For work-life balance, it's important to have hobbies and interests outside of work.

Taking part in activities that make you happy, help you feel fulfilled, and help you grow as a person can help balance the pressures of work and make your life more satisfying and well-rounded.

Example: Find hobbies or talents you're really interested in and make time for them regularly. Whether you play a musical instrument, paint, farm, or play sports, doing any of these things will make you feel happy and fulfilled.

2. Building relationships that matter:

Having a good balance between work and life means taking care of important ties with family, friends, and loved ones. Putting time and effort into keeping and improving these relationships is good for your general happiness and sense of fulfilment.

Example: Spend valuable time with people you care about, whether it's over meals, trips, or just regular chats. Do things that bring people together, like family game nights, dates with a partner, or get-togethers with friends. Getting to know these people and keeping in touch with them will bring you support and happiness.

3. Seeking Novel Experiences:

Seeking out new things to do and getting out of your comfort zone gives your life more variety and energy. Exploring new places, trying new things, or learning new skills can be a fun way to take a break from work and help you grow as a person.

Example: Plan trips or outings on a regular basis to learn about new places and countries. If you want to learn a new skill or hobby, you can go to camps or classes. Accept chances to grow as a person and push yourself to do things that are out of your comfort zone.

Conclusion:

Achieving a good balance between work and personal life is an ongoing process that takes conscious effort and self-awareness. By using the tips and routines in this chapter, you can make self-care a top priority, take care of your relationships, and work on your own growth and happiness. Remember that finding balance is an ongoing process that changes over time. To keep a good work-life balance, you need to regularly review and change your approach.

Chapter 12

Digital Detox and Mindful Tech Use

In the modern age we live in now, technology is a big part of both our personal and professional lives. But using technology too much and being online all the time can cause stress, distraction, and a feeling of being too busy. In this chapter, we look at routines for digital detox and mindful technology use. These are ways to have a better relationship with technology and find balance in the digital world.

Recognising the Impact of Digital Overload

1. The Effects of Too Much Technology:

Too much time in front of a computer, frequent alerts, and too much information can hurt our mental and emotional health. It can make you less productive, less able to concentrate, less able to sleep well, and more stressed out.

Example: Imagine a person who is always checking their phone, answering work emails outside of office hours, and looking through social media whenever they have spare time. Over time, this kind of behaviour can cause more worry, lower work quality, and a lack of presence in personal relationships.

2. Understanding Digital Addiction:

Digital addiction is when someone uses technology too much and can't stop it. It can make people lose control over how they use technology, put off their tasks, and hurt many parts of their lives, such as their relationships, work performance, and general health.

Example: Think about a person who has trouble turning off their devices, who is always checking social media, and who gets anxious when they are away from technology. This over-dependence on technology can make it hard for them to do important things and keep healthy limits.

Implementing Digital Detox Rituals

1. Creating Digital-Free Zones:

Set aside times or places in your day where you won't use technology. Make places or times where you turn off your devices on purpose and focus on being in the moment.

Example: Set aside the dining room or bedroom as places where you can't use technology. Try not to use devices at meals or before bed. Use this time to have a chat, eat a meal without being distracted, or just relax without electronics.

2. Setting Boundaries and Limitations:

Set clear restrictions and limits around technology use to stop people from spending too much time in front of screens and to encourage thoughtful involvement. Set times to check emails, look through social media, and do other online activities.

Example: Make a plan for how you use technology, like only checking your email at certain times of the day instead of all the time. Set limits on how much time you spend on social media, and use apps or tools that keep track of and limit computer time. By setting limits, you can get back in control of technology and make time for more important things.

3. Engaging in Digital Sabbaticals:

Getting away from technology for a set amount of time can help you recover and improve your mental health. Take "digital sabbaticals," where you purposely spend time away from your devices and on things you can do without them.

Example: Plan a weekend trip or day trip where you leave your devices behind and fully enjoy nature, a hobby, or valuable time with family and friends. Use this time to rest, get back in touch with yourself and others, and see things from a new angle.

Practising Mindful Technology Use

1. Developing a Digital Awareness:

Mindful technology use means becoming aware of how we use technology and making mindful decisions about how and when to use digital devices. It lets people use technology on purpose instead of mindlessly scrolling or being constantly distracted.

Example: Before you use a device, take a moment to think about what you want to do. Ask yourself if the action fits with your ideals, goals, or well-being. Practise being in the moment and fully involved in what you're doing instead of doing other things or looking mindlessly.

2. Creating a Digital Environment:

Control your digital environment by curating. This will improve your health. Think about the apps, messages, and online material you use and make choices that will make your digital life more positive and uplifting.

Example: Unsubscribe from email services you don't need, turn off or mute messages that aren't important, and organise your files and folders to clear up your digital area. Follow accounts and interact with material that fits with your hobbies, values, and personal growth.

3. Intentional Social Media Usage:

When used wisely, social media can be a great way to meet new people, get ideas, and learn. Develop good social media habits, such as reading slowly, setting time limits, and interacting with important content and groups.

Example: Set a limit on how much time you spend on social media each day and use apps or tools that keep track of how much time you spend on social media. Follow accounts that make you feel good and inspire you, and unfollow or hide accounts that make you feel bad or make you compare yourself to others. Talk about things that matter and help internet groups in a good way.

Conclusion:

Finding a good balance in our digital lives is important for our health, happiness, and work. By using digital detox routines and being more aware of how we use technology, we can regain control over our relationship with it, reduce stress, and make room for more important experiences that don't involve technology. Remember that making healthy digital habits is an ongoing process that takes self-awareness, discipline, and purpose. By putting digital well-being first, you can find a better balance between your personal life and the digital world.

"The way you care for yourself should be as special as you are."

Chapter 13

Rituals for Financial Well-being

A healthy and happy life isn't complete without good financial health. In Chapter 13, "Rituals for Financial Well-Being," we look at ways to build good money habits, set personal goals, and handle costs well through rituals. By doing these things on a regular basis, busy workers can get a handle on their money and work towards long-term financial safety and success.

Creating Healthy Financial Habits

1. Changing Your Mind About Money:

Building good money habits starts with having a positive and powerful attitude about money. It means having a good relationship with money, changing beliefs that hold you back, and welcoming wealth and financial freedom.

Example: Start by thinking about what you think and feel about money. Find any negative or limiting thoughts you have and try to turn them into positive and powerful mantras. Accept the idea that you can have a lot of money and be financially stable.

2. Practising Conscious Spending:

Conscious buying means that you think about how you spend your money before you do it. To do this, you need to think about what you value, make sure your buying matches your ideals, and practise "mindful consumption."

Example: Before you buy something, ask yourself if it fits with your beliefs and helps your well-being as a whole. Think about whether it's a need or a want and whether it will make you happy in the long run. Don't buy things on the spur of the moment, and give yourself time to think before making big financial choices.

3. Building an Emergency Fund:

An emergency fund is a key part of being financially stable. It gives you a safety net for unexpected costs or financial losses, and it lowers the stress that comes with money problems. To build an emergency fund, you need to save money regularly and be responsible with your money.

Example: Set a clear plan for your emergency fund, like saving enough money to cover your living costs for three to six months. Make a budget that sets aside a certain amount of your monthly income for savings. Set up automatic payments to a different savings account to save money without having to think about it.

Setting Personal Goals for Growth

1. Defining Financial Goals:

Setting clear, important financial goals helps you figure out what to do with your money and gives you the motivation to act. Whether you're saving for a down payment, paying off debt, or investing for retirement, setting your goals helps you make a plan for financial success.

Example: Set cash goals for the short, medium, and long runs. Be clear about how much money you want to save or how much debt you want to pay off, and give yourself a deadline for each goal. Write them down and look at them often to keep yourself on track and inspired.

2. Investing in Personal Growth:

Putting money into your own growth and development is a great way to improve your financial situation. It means getting new skills, learning more, and improving your ability to make money.

Example: Figure out where you want to improve yourself or your career. Think about taking classes, going to events, and getting licences that will help you reach your goals. Invest in building skills that will make you more valuable on the job market or give you new chances to move up in your career.

3. Seeking Professional Financial Advice:

If you talk to a professional about your finances, they can give you valuable information and help you make smart choices. Financial advisors can give advice on how to spend, plan for retirement, minimise taxes, and handle money in general.

Example: Do some research and find a reliable financial advisor who specialises in the areas that are important to your financial goals. Set up a meeting with them to talk about your finances and goals and to get advice on how to make a personalised financial plan.

Budgeting and Managing Expenses

1. Creating a Personal Budget:

A personal budget is one of the most important tools for handling costs, keeping track of income, and making sure you don't spend more than you make. It gives you a clear picture of your finances, so you can make smart choices about how you spend your money.

Example: Start by keeping track of your income and spending for a month to see how you spend your money. Use a planning app or a worksheet to make a monthly budget that sets aside money for necessities, savings, paying off debt, and spending on things you want. Review and change your budget often to reflect changes in your financial situation.

2. Minimising Debt and Managing Credit:

Debt can have a big effect on your finances, so it's important to figure out how to deal with it and use credit in a smart way. Less financial stress and more financial freedom can come from having less debt and a good handle on credit.

Example: Make a plan to pay off your bills by putting the ones with the highest interest rates first or using the debt snowball or debt explosion methods. If it fits with your financial goals, you might want to try to get lower interest rates or combine your bills. Pay your bills on time, keep your credit card amounts low, and don't get into debt that you don't need to.

3. Practising Smart Spending Habits:

Having smart spending habits means making choices that help you get the most out of your money and what you spend. It includes things like shopping around, haggling over prices, and looking for ways to save on everyday costs.

Example: Before making a big buy, do some research to find the best deals or savings. Compare the prices at different stores or web marketplaces. When it makes sense, you should try to get a better price, especially for services like insurance or energy bills. Look for ways to save money on normal costs, like planning meals, making choices that use less energy, or using coupons.

Conclusion:

Getting to a good place financially is a process that takes deliberate actions and a long-term view. Busy professionals can take control of their finances and work towards a safe and successful future by putting in place routines that help them build good money habits, set personal goals, and manage their costs well. Remember that taking small steps regularly can lead to big changes in your finances.

Chapter 14

Establishing a Self-Care Network

In our journey to cracking the self-care code, it's important to have a network of people who understand and value self-care. In this chapter, we look at routines for building a supportive self-care network. We talk about how important it is to surround yourself with people who share your values and can encourage you, hold you accountable, and inspire you. Busy workers can build a strong support system for themselves by making important connections and taking care of their relationships.

Creating a Supportive Circle

1. Finding People with Similar Ideas:

The first step in building a network of people who can help you take care of yourself is to find people who share your beliefs and commitment to self-care. Find people who put their health first, share your hobbies, and know how important it is to take care of yourself in a busy work life.

Example: Take part in online and live self-care clubs or groups. Go to classes, lectures, or retreats that focus on your health and happiness. Join social or business groups where you can meet people who care about the same things you do.

2. Developing Genuine Connections:

To make real bonds, you need open conversation, trust, and the ability to be vulnerable. Build connections with people who support, understand, and don't judge each other. Share how you take care of yourself and listen to what others have to say.

Example: Set up regular check-ins with the people who help you, either in person or online. Share what you do to take care of yourself, what you've learned, and what you've accomplished. Actively listen and give support and guidance to those around you. Have important talks that help you learn more about each other's needs for self-care.

3. Establishing Accountability Partnerships:

Accountability with friends can be a very important part of your journey towards self-care. By making goals together, supporting each other, and holding each other responsible, you can strengthen your commitment to self-care and make your routines more consistent.

Example: Find people in your network who care about self-care and want to form responsible relationships. Set clear goals for self-care, and make a plan for checking in and keeping track of progress. Help you stay committed to your self-care habits by giving you support, motivation, and gentle reminders.

Emotional Support and Empathy

1. Getting better at active listening:

Active listening is a key skill for developing understanding and helping other people feel better. It means paying full attention, not judging, and really knowing how other people feel and what they've been through.

Example: Active hearing means keeping eye contact, showing with words and body language that you are interested, and not talking over the speaker. Validate the other person's thoughts and feelings and show care and understanding without giving help or answers right away.

2. Offering Emotional Support:

Emotional support means being there for someone when they are going through a hard time, giving them comfort, and giving them a safe place to talk about their feelings. By creating a helpful setting, you build a network of people who can help each other feel better emotionally.

Example: If someone in your support network needs to talk or let off steam, be open and easy to reach. Give words of support, comfort, and approval. Make a place where people can talk about their problems and feelings without fear of being judged.

3. Practising Self-Compassion in Relationships:

Self-compassion also affects how we interact with people in our support network. It means being kind, understanding, and accepting of ourselves and others. By practising self-compassion in our relationships, we create a setting that is nurturing and helpful.

Example: Self-compassion means being kind to yourself by accepting your flaws and the flaws of others. Don't judge or criticise, but offer help and understanding. Encourage self-care practises in your network by showing others how to be kind to themselves and put their own health first.

Collaborative Self-Care Practises

1. Group Self-Care Activities:

Engaging in group self-care activities not only brings people together but also lets them share stories and help each other. Self-care practises that involve others can include things like working out as a group, going on wellness vacations, or taking part in art classes.

Example: Set up regular group self-care tasks with people in your network of support. Set up a walk, a cooking class, or a time to meditate together. Do things that help the group, so that everyone can learn from the experience.

2. Peer Support Groups:

Peer support groups are a way for people to get together, share their stories, and help each other in an organised way. These groups provide a safe place to talk about problems, ask for help, and celebrate progress.

Example: Make or join a peer support group that is centred on self-care and well-being. Meet up regularly to talk about your own experiences, talk about ways to take care of yourself, and offer support. Use the group's combined knowledge and experiences to improve how you take care of yourself.

3. Collaboration in Goal Setting:

In collective goal setting, you and your support network work together to set and reach self-care goals. By telling others about your goals, how you're doing, and obstacles, you can get ideas, drive, and a sense of responsibility.

Example: Set up goal-setting meetings with the people who help you. Encourage people to share their goals for self-care and set up a system that will help them keep track of their progress.

Encourage people, celebrate their successes, and help them when they run into problems.

Conclusion:

As a busy professional, building a self-care network of people who can help you is a powerful way to improve your self-care journey. By creating a supportive group, developing empathy and mental support, and working together on self-care, you can make important links and create a healthy environment. Keep in mind that the strength of your self-care network depends on the quality of your relationships and how much you all want to put self-care first.

Chapter 15

Maintaining Your Self-Care Journey

Sometimes it can be hard to keep up with self-care rituals when there are so many things to do at work and in life. In this last Chapter of my book "The Self-Care Code", you'll learn about routines that can help you stay on track with your self-care journey, with a focus on long-term stability, getting past problems, and building resilience. You can make self-care an important part of your life by finding ways to stay inspired and strong.

Fostering Consistency and Accountability

1. Establishing Rituals and Routines:

Self-care practises need to be done the same way every time. By making traditions and patterns, you create a structure that helps you take care of yourself regularly. These habits are like magnets that remind you to put your health first, even when you have a lot going on.

Example: Set specific times for self-care tasks, like meditating in the morning, writing in the evening, or exercising once a week. Make a plan to include these practises in your everyday life, and don't change your mind about them.

2. Tracking Progress and Celebrating Milestones:

Keeping track of your self-care journey lets you see how far you've come and where you can improve. It also gives you a chance to enjoy milestones and recognise how your self-care practises have helped your general health.

Example: Keep a self-care log or use a mobile app to keep track of the things you do, how you feel about them, and how far you've come. Set goals for yourself and have a party when you reach them. Think about the good things that have happened and use them to keep going on your self-care journey.

3. Engaging an Accountability Partner or Support System:

Having accountability friends or a network of people who care about you can help you keep up with self-care practises. When you tell other people about your goals, obstacles, and successes, you feel a sense of responsibility and support, which keeps you motivated and accountable.

Example: Find a partner who will hold you accountable, or join a self-care group where people can help and inspire each other.

Check-in with your partner or group often to share news, ask for advice, or give support. You are more likely to stick with your self-care journey if you encourage responsibility.

Overcoming Obstacles and Building Resilience

1. Identifying and Addressing Barriers:

On your path to self-care, you will run into problems and obstacles. For your self-care practises to last, you need to figure out what could get in the way and come up with ways to get around them. You can stay determined and strong in the face of problems if you deal with them before they happen.

Example: Think about the things that have gotten in the way of your self-care habits in the past. Plan for possible problems, like work goals, family obligations, or a lack of motivation, and come up with answers ahead of time. Make plans for what to do if something goes wrong so that you can still take care of yourself even when things are hard.

2. Prioritising Self-Care in Busy Periods:

When you're busy at work or in life, you might be tempted to put off taking care of yourself. But it's during these times that taking care of yourself is even more important. Finding ways to take care of yourself even when you're busy is important if you want to stay healthy.

Example: Find small bits of time throughout the day to do quick self-care activities, like focused breathing techniques or short walks. Break up chores into pieces that you can handle, and plan time for yourself in between. When you can, give jobs to other people or hire them out so you have more time for self-care.

3. Building Resilience and Self-Compassion:

Resilience is the ability to get back on your feet after a loss and keep an upbeat attitude. You can get through challenges, failures, and times when you question yourself if you learn to be resilient and kind to yourself.

Example: You can practise self-compassion by accepting your flaws and being kind and understanding to yourself. Develop resilience by practising mindfulness, saying good things to yourself, and asking for help from your self-care network. Think about what you've learned from your mistakes and use them as opportunities for growth.

Evolving Self-Care Practises and Adaptability
1. Embracing Evolving Needs and Interests:

Your wants and goals for self-care may change over time, and it's important to be open to these changes. Your self-care journey will continue to be satisfying and useful if you check in on it often and change your habits to fit your changing needs.

Example: Think about the ways you take care of yourself now and decide how successful they are and how well they fit with your present goals and interests. Explore new ways to take care of yourself, like new hobbies or ways to stay healthy. Be willing to try new things and change your routines as needed.

2. Continual Learning and Exploration:

Self-care is a process of learning and discovering that never ends. By looking for new information, ideas, and points of view, you can make your self-care practises better and keep them interesting.

Example: Personal growth can be done by reading books, listening to podcasts, going to classes, or taking online courses that focus on well-being and self-care. Attend workshops or gatherings about self-care or well-being to learn more and get advice from people who know a lot about the subject.

3. Integrating Self-Care into Your Lifestyle:

The ultimate objective is to make self-care a normal and unavoidable part of your daily life. By making self-care a regular part of your life, you can make sure it lasts and get the most out of it.

Review your daily habits and look for places where you can add self-care practises. Include self-care in things you already do, like practising mindfulness on your commute or being grateful at mealtimes. Self-care should be a top priority, so set aside time each day for it, even if it means changing your plan.

Conclusion:

Chapter 15 talks about how important it is to keep going on the self-care journey by being consistent, getting past problems, and being open to change. You can make sure that self-care stays an important part of your busy work life by setting up habits and routines, staying accountable, building resilience, and being open to your changing needs. Remember that self-care is an ongoing process, and by putting your health first, you give yourself the power to do well in both your personal and professional life.

*****

Conclusion

It is all too easy to neglect our own health and place self-care on the back burner in the midst of our busy lives. However, the reality is that you deserve to prioritise yourself. You have the right to cultivate a nourishing, fulfilling, and balanced existence.

This book is a guide, a compass that will lead you to the rituals that will revitalise your mind, body, and spirit. It is time to rewrite the narrative of your chaotic professional life, foster it with self-care, and develop a code that uplifts and empowers you.

Together, let's embark on this transformative journey in which self-care becomes the foundation of your success, contentment, and well-being. You are deserving of every second, every breath, and every ritual that will help you flourish. It is time to crack the self-care code and reveal your finest self.

Congratulations on decoding **The Self-Care Code,** or I must say at this time, The Code of Success. You have opened the door to a more balanced, joyous, and meaningful life by prioritising self-care and applying these transforming rituals and tactics. Remember that self-care is a lifelong endeavour that needs dedication and self-compassion. Accept the key rituals presented in this book and allow them to guide you to long-term well-being and success.

May you always carve out time, create space, and extend compassion towards caring for yourself, for it is through self-care that you can truly thrive.

"Now is the time to take action, break the code, and prioritise your self-care rituals to unlock an enhanced version of yourself."

The End

Made in the USA
Middletown, DE
15 April 2025

74324837R00083